Demented Dreamz:
Deprived Without a Reason

By: Elizabeth J. Crowl

Cover Illustrated by: Brittany Crowl

This book is dedicated to my siblings that I love
more than anyone in this world

Kirk Jr.

Brittany

Tyler

Jamie

Jesse

To the following three teachers that helped
me so much with my book and myself

Holly Bantum

Luisa Gunther

Kristie Sigler

Also to special friends that helped me during some of the worst times

Jacqui Frazier

Carla Lycan

And in loving memory of two dear friends that passed away
last year that were very close to my heart

Gloria "Mama Gloria" Cirullo

Michael "Big Mike" Kerr

Introduction

My name is Elizabeth Crowl and I am the composer of the poems you are about to read. Although I am not an expert in psychology or poetry, I would say I am skilled on how children deal with situations thrown at them that no one should have to deal with. Anyone who has experienced this type of life may agree with me or they may have had a different reaction towards their own life. These poems do not represent every child that has had a similar experience; these particular poems represent my feelings on circumstances I was faced with throughout the past ten years. I started writing when I was 15 years old and my first poem is in this book titled "Her." This was the only coping method I had during my teenage years that was not self destructive.

As I got older I started doing abusive things to myself because writing no longer helped me cope as more tragedies came to light. I stopped writing for a year and a half during this destructive time in my life. After destroying my self esteem as much as I could, I had a handful of people that tried to push me in the right direction. The one lesson I learned was that if you aren't ready to lead a righteous life no one can make you. Finally after years and years of directly hurting myself and indirectly harming others, I was ready for baby steps. I was learning how to overcome my addictions and how to make better decisions for myself. I had to learn how to treat myself as well as I tried to treat other people.

I needed to grow up and figure out that I had to gain strength on my own, but I also grasped an idea about my poems. The plan occurred to me that if I published my collection of poems maybe I could show another person that I have been there and know where they are right now. Perhaps this could be the starting point for someone to see that life will not be this way forever. I am not trying to say that life will always be extraordinary for everyone, but once you plummet to rock bottom you have to decide to stand up and work your way up or to stay down there. I can imagine someone reading this right now thinking there is no way it will ever get better, but it can. I have been there and I know how hard it is to do it by yourself. I had to do it because I was sick of waiting around for someone to hold my hand and lead the way.

My parents didn't care and no matter how unfair it was, nothing would ever change that. But if I would have sat around waiting for new parents, I still wouldn't have any and I would have wasted a lot of time. Throughout my life so far, I have realized one thing my parents will never be able to take from me. That is the love I now have for myself and the love I have for my siblings. No one can carry the weight of the world by themselves and I know that it is so much harder to listen to this when you are carrying it all alone, but you need to ask for help. People will go so far out of their way if they recognize you need support, but you have to let someone know. People cannot just guess who is in trouble; you need to reach out first so they can reach back.

I hope my book will inspire someone to stand up and not be content with walking on the bottom for the rest of their life. I am not 100% healed from all of the ordeals that happened in my life, but through counseling and helping others I am making progress. I just hope this book reaches someone that has felt alone with no one there to reach out to. I have an email address, located in the back of this book, you can go to where you can ask questions and leave a comment or you can tell me your own story. I also have a web address that can be accessed for anyone that is currently dealing with any of the issues talked about in this book. Thank you.

Caution: The book you are about to start reading

Has crooked thoughts about death and not succeeding

If you are an upbeat person put tears on reserve

Emotion will spring from every muscle, bone, and nerve

Twisted feelings and unconventional methods are being used

All thoughts coming from a mind that was excessively abused

This all started with horrible dreams and demented thoughts

Images so unreal that words were created and put into plot

Life never ends up being simple or what it may seem

If your every emotion is in full blast, you may now enter…

Demented Dreamz

"Getting Closer"

Try to pull me in and against my heart I will run away

One day I will open up to a person and not paper, but that's not today

Innocent eyes were tainted long ago in this translucent world

When I was an adult by mind, yet physically a little girl

Care and concern became a wish and fell last on our family list

Hoping dad wasn't drunk and hoping mom would not raise her fist

Beer was in the refrigerator without food on the table

Mom could afford crack, but nurturing became a fable

The kids had as much as my older brother and I could give

All of the kids pulling together because otherwise we would not live

Lunch money was only something the younger ones were handed

That was something my brother and I worked for and demanded

We would steal if we had to, but we didn't want that for them

We didn't want children services examining our lives that were so grim

We grew up with roots of bitterness and mentalities so rigid

Dad was intoxicated and mom was high and livid

I have kept all of this bottled up hoping no one would ever notice

We never worked through our issues because no one had ever shown us

Then someone stepped in and tried to take away my tears

Getting closer to me and realizing my parents were my fears

Everyone looks down on us without knowing who we are

That is why I keep running, running away so far

"Her"

Her eyes were black and meaningless, so very dark
She was thin and skinny like a model superstar
I was conflicted on her real mental stage
I look into my eyes and they are soaked with rage
My ability was put to the test
I wish I would fall into an eternal rest
Life will never be the same
My family torn and scarred with shame
Why does life have to be this bad
My childhood here and gone in a flash
What did I do to deserve all of this
Funny and cheerful are the feelings I miss
Mothers are supposed to be there for you
To love and admire anything that you do
People tell me they can understand
None of them could cope with this horror land
I was never ready for adulthood yet
I was not ready to make that step
I was waiting for a sign from above
Ever since she left and lost my love
Age was a battle she thought she could fight
Then drugs took her over with all their might
But she lost the battle before it begun
Destroying lives was the only battle she won

"Out of Sight, Out of Mind"

Starting over once, twice, I may have lost count

Failure is running through my veins, an extensive amount

Some may say you can only move up when there is no way down

I heard that years ago and I am still stuck out of bounds

No one ever asked if I wanted to give up my dreams

Now I am ganged up on and I wasn't picked on either team

Everyone acts like I don't have any rights

Once again I bought my ticket and missed my flight

I cannot take it anymore when I am put down and do not resist

I will close my eyes, tears falling, wishing I didn't exist

Pretending my issues were false, so I never really faced them

Leaving the candle in my soul glowing forever so dim

My life moved fast like I blinked and it was behind

No one waited for me, out of sight and out of mind

"Empty Seat"

Passions so truly inspiring, no words could equate

With new memories evolving, no others could relate

Last minute acceptance could not add up to this feeling

Then slowly, a little bit of her soul started peeling

Something must have happened, everything completely reversed

The mentality of a healthy being became malnourished

The stone of her eyes, no twinkle or glisten

Realizing is a must, yet no one will listen

Now I say to those that think I've become solid stone

I have emotions, I can feel, I can even write poems

Watching a movie I can laugh, I can be captivated

When I am hurt I cry, if I get picked on I get aggravated

I am not frozen, if you cut me open I will bleed

The same admirations and morals most people believe

Mine may be slightly hazy for what my past will reveal

If it were my choice my mother's identity would remain concealed

She left us here so that the world could have our defeat

In my mind she is dead now, just another empty seat

"Alone"

No one around or to be seen
A place of peace and harmony
With a clear mind and a relaxing thought
No longer impatient or feeling distraught
A world of its own where feelings are never wrong
A mysterious place where I feel like I belong
Not always wanting to have everyone around
Thinking to myself and not hearing a sound
Thinking through the days and recapping in silence
Replaying the hours and trying to forget the violence
Needing time to absorb this broken family in disguise
Wishing I did not hate the reality behind these eyes

"Silent Tears"

Liquid drops of nothing falling from my face
Calm and quiet surroundings, I am unfamiliar with this place
Wanting to be happy is what created all of these tears
Flowing from this river that has been endless for many years
The last cry for help has been demolished and severed
Maybe because I could not find that best friend forever
Now I am getting hasty as my heart fills with anger
Indecisive in my ways as my mind leads me to danger
The cycle started all over again with hate and then sadness
Once again silent tears start falling and no one can see my madness
Nobody understands me because I live with mixed emotions
Tears that led to puddles that turned into enormous oceans
Wondering how fast so many people's lives have changed
Why the person that brought us here left us estranged
Some may think these beliefs are like walking through life blind
But I only have these thoughts because no one was ever kind

"SSDD"

A train wreck inside, twenty people died
A motherless child, I remember when he cried
Hallways of shadows, darkness in my mind
A world so unstable and yet so divine
Very little money, working for minimum wage
A scared and unruly child, now locked in a cage
This tiny space is empty, but it feels so cluttered
A toy for you to play with, then thrown in the gutter
By age thirteen all grown up living like a mother
Little sister is now mine along with two little brothers
Dad is acting tough without a tear drop to see
So my brothers bring their artwork to my sister and me
Trying to stay calm instead of acting like a fool
Not able to deal with it all, so I dropped out of school
I didn't want to quit because we had made it this far
But the only thing to show for it was an ice cold heart
It never thawed out since I had lost the sense to care
Now I lie in my casket with a lifeless stare

1.2 Million Students drop out of school each year

Only 50% of students at inner city schools graduate

Without a Reflection"

A fear of reflection to see inside
Waiting for these feelings to become another lie
Scared of my true colors shining right past my face
Not wanting to go back, not again to that place
Holding my childhood picture close to my heart so dear
A look too close with no reflection in the mirror
With more episodes going on and life at the most
Another rock n roller is dying from an overdose
Confused on how to take the next steps forward
I guess I just got used to sitting in the corner
Reaching out a hand for someone to come and help
Once again, no one is there so I will do it by myself
My mind is racing and I need to relax
Instead I hit the wall and fall on my back
Then I waited for your embrace that I never received
Yet my hopes expired before I was ever deceived
I've been let down more then a handful of times
With a heart that used to be wide open until openly denied

"My Candle"

You were my candle that was never meant to go out

Growing brighter if I were upset or wanted to pout

One day my candle started glowing a shade too dim

I knew it would never burn the same way again

Trying to savor that light as long as I could

Maybe I did not try as hard as I should

I remember the day the wick stopped burning

My fifteenth birthday, the whole world stopped turning

You did not show up or even try to call

Piece by piece my entire world started to fall

Every once in a while I still see the flame flicker

But the light dies down never getting any thicker

Sometimes I wonder how I would feel if you were here to talk to

Then I remember my candle blew out and the breath came from you

"Turn Away"

I have known you for so long, but I don't know who you are
I am standing right next to you, but you feel so far
A disappearance happened, no one could figure out why
Fading more and more as each day passes by
Hoping the good memories are not as dominant anymore
Letting every aspect of that time escape my core
Hearing words that lied because the inevitable happened
Sitting here without you with fingers just tapping
As kids we would get in trouble and I would take the blame
Now to have ever said you were my best friend brings me shame
The only time you open up is if you have had a beer
You call your parents alcoholics; have a look in the mirror
Thank you for adding to the failure I have become
The insignificant in which society shunned
You walked all over me without a second thought
Doing drugs without a care, never concerned about being caught
At this time too much has occurred for this friendship to stay
I leave you without a glance as I forever walk away

4 in 10 children who begin drinking before age 15 become alcoholics

"Missing a Link"

Drinking for the sleep that I am deprived of at night
Hung-over I stumble around, such an afternoon delight
The sun starts to come up and I can't figure out why
I cannot fall asleep no matter how tight I close my eyes
Trying to clear my head, yet more confusion sets in
Similar to the previous hours the cycle starts all over again
I take photographs to keep things stored in my memory
But it never fades because I am haunted by my own treachery
At one point in time I had words that were exchanged
Acting out towards myself, yet I don't feel deranged
Without sleep, I have forever to play this little game
To wake up tomorrow and it will still be the same
Like a split personality I do not know how to behave
Fighting with myself through writing, yet nothing real to say
Happiness… a word, a fight, or a rhetorical question
Trying to lead a pure life, but I was only taught deception

"Abandoned"

Scared, a noise, a face in the darkness
Tears, emptiness, she could not feel any less
Denial, a question, hate had broken its seal
Anger, hypertension, how hot she must feel
Depression, tears of sorrow, saturated in emotion
Acceptance, realization, leaving wounds and corrosion
Images in her mind slowly leaving only to return again
Leaving her unstable in a world predominantly foreign
Questions and thoughts without an adult to be heard of
No longer living as a child, more of a soldier rejecting love
Sleepless nights wondering where her parents were
Bewildered as all of her emotions started to concur
Left behind without an ending like a fairy tale book
No one saw beneath the surface or took a second look
She was not just upset about the situation at hand
She just never found anyone that could even partially understand

"Can You See Us"

Can you see us standing in front of you

We are right here and cannot be anymore true

When was the last time you were clean

Not for a while, since you call us names so obscene

You never tried to help us, you just caused less bliss

I try to count the caring people, not enough to list

Trials and suffering all through the time we knew each other

The first set of all knowing tears, cried by my little brothers

No one heard our cries, no one heard our screams

Living life in safety, but only in our dreams

Please do not wake us, do not pinch our skin

Let us dream a little longer before the nightmare begins

I run through the halls to look for help, but no one showed me the light

Now our bodies become soldiers, ignoring love and accepting the fight

We have no fear because no one could ever hurt us more then you

We accepted your addictions and did what we had to do

No child should ever have to feel abandoned or left to suffer

The most pain ever felt caused by their own mother

"Brain Damage"

I can only try to understand why you were wrong
How was I supposed to know it would take this long
Accepting everything you threw at me with your guilt trip
Causing pain right down the center where my heart ripped
Verbal abuse to cut through with so much damage
A final cut that the most skilled doctor could not bandage
Swelling in my skull with no room to breathe
Deadly, no one is left and now the spirits are free
Pieces of you floating about in my hollow zone
The echoes getting louder with your abusive tone
The beat with one and two, but I cannot hear
The dance of the renegades that all of you fear
One lesson to learn that is heavier then stone
Taught to you since youth, so that is all that is known
Break away from everything that was brought to mind
Living life cynically, but trying not to cross the line
Fear inhabited inside my former soul that was cursed
With drops of anguish falling until completely submerged

"Please Just Listen"

Memories erase because they were never linking

Scars across my body because I could not stop thinking

Keeping my mouth shut because there was something I couldn't say

About how I cried after wiping my baby brother's tears away

Holding him close, because no one else had the time

Hearing mom leave and knowing she left to do a line

I try so hard to keep us together, but the situation is rough

Holding my head high because for the kids I must be tough

Talking to the walls now because I don't have any friends

Then I called a meeting for my soul, but nobody attends

My mind has escaped and my heart is gone

I lost everything now, so please just play my song

Listen to the words and try to see my mentality

I must be talking to myself again, which leads me to a fatality

Forgetful as I was I lost the runaway train

Breathless through the night because I drowned in the rain

I hope I will not be judged for all of my sins

I get confounded; my mind retracts, as this poem plays again

"The Forgotten"

With a conscience that speaks loud and clear

Days of past crimes, recounting every tear

Regret is not an issue because life is too short

Learning from all the time I had to spend in court

The past is true and my scars are the reminders

The lack of guidance while I was writing in my binder

Someone once tried to grab my hand, but I let go

Remembering in this misplaced mind I was never told no

I realized you were in the palm of my hand

You tried to open me up again, but this time I made a stand

Conviction from the explosion, the life, and the lesson

Bloodshed and cultivation was my natural obsession

As a result of poverty and a violent life there lies a gun

But if you die, who would care, would there even be one

"Black River"

Hatred that flows in your veins and turns your mind black
Never letting up, because with evil you can never relax
So intense the blood starts to boil and spurt out bits of hate
Only the contender can now determine his or her own fate
This river seems to flow forever because I cannot see the end
Eventually the river dies down and hatred starts to descend
Murderers have this passion that is darker then any other
Getting a high off adrenaline for making someone suffer
The sane can only wonder, the religious not understand
The way evildoers feel with blood dripping from their hand
They get the pulse and take it out on everybody else
Not me though, I take it out on myself

"Mystery of My History"

At night the frozen tear drops fall from my face
Solid ice is freezing, but my heart had to be replaced
Certain songs bring back the few highlights in my mind
As a young child I walked around with eyes so blind
How did I not see what was happening right in front of me
Mom was so secretive and she was stealing all of our money
Then the detectives showed up and told dad what I already knew
'Your wife is on drugs and she is screwing a drug dealer, too'
The family did not believe me when I told them about her
It wasn't until the cops said it that the family concurred
I was the first one to find out she was cheating
And for that mommy dearest gave me a brutal beating
Sometimes I think that I am the only kid that understands
It's like everyone else lives in a fairytale land
I just want this to be over and start a brand new day
But these memories keep haunting me, they are here to stay

"Fading Faces"

Sitting on a shelf until she would come to play
Just like the last time, she was not home to stay
Never wanting to be her puppets, although that's what they became
Thinking she would finally settle, that was her demented game
Sitting and waiting, the only possession they had was dust
Everyone left them and as a result they lack trust
If she did not want these toys then someone else may have
Wishful thinking is the only constant they ever had
Anytime someone started to pick them up they showed attachment
This never lasted long because the possessor would feel the entrapment
The only thing these toys needed was a loving person to care
Someone to play with them, give them boundaries, and just be there
Being stuffed would be much easier for the absence of emotion
Never feeling scared when their parents started a commotion
No one ever attempted to rescue these kids made into toys
It would be a lot with two rigid girls and three angry boys
Then their mom just dropped them completely, ending their story
Shattered in a million pieces dying without glory

"Rain"

The candle light dimmed and the wind was roaring
The night was quiet with creatures soaring
The clock was ticking louder with every tick tock
Her eyes were focused, glued to this clock
The hands were going the wrong direction
Perhaps it was just a misconception
Eerie was the night, lightning now flashing
The winds are mightier, I can hear things crashing
A single rain drop on the window rolls down so slow
The sky grew darker leaving much time until the afterglow
Just as the night seemed to become disturbingly quiet
Nature's wonders came together and started an all out riot
Shingles were ripping off and the house was shaking
Windows were rattling and tree branches were breaking
The storm of the century with more deaths then ever
Curses of having a mind made up of stormy weather

"Waking up Schizophrenic"

Voices and screams circling around my thoughts
Talking to me and justifying the fights that were fought
Consciously playing games with figments of imagination
Legally insane caused by Mommy's own creation
Losing the grasp of all that used to seem sane
Letting my guard down on the enemies terrain
If you aren't afraid to die then no one can scare you
They pull out a gun and I tell them 'I dare you'
See if they are true about shooting you that very minute
Even if they shoot you at least you knew going in it
Counseling could not help me be tame, I need life support
I ask myself a question and my brain instinctively retorts
Flying by one million miles an hour and still growing
Sleepless nightmares, I am fearful of not knowing
Criticism of my own satire with every word
Terrified even further because more voices are being heard
Louder and stronger the dancing echoes have become
Pleading to unlock my eyes for emotional freedom
A seizure without motion from the mental overload
As nightmares and reality cease at an open crossroad

1 in every 5 Americans will be affected by a mental disorder this year

"Unknown Soldier"

The rain of the enemy with a face I cannot see
Following me around, but this truly cannot be
You have done something to me that was unforgivable
I try and try to hurt you, but you seem to be invincible
You have caused me much shame leaving me in disgrace
I want to see you at this moment; I want to see your face
Show me the person that always haunts my dreams
Lining up with other people killing me in teams
Cutting me down slowly until I am completely finished
Waking up dazed to find my dreams had already diminished
I want to see the one who helped cut my self esteem
The reason I chose not to love and never want to succeed
For living without love has been like breathing in ice
Although it was my choice I do not want to pay the price
How dare you for hiding and being the reason I am shaking
I said I could beat you, but apparently I was faking
I want to see the disciple that was sent by the enemy
Then a look in the mirror showed me the face I could not see

"Dreamer"

Sorrow for sorrow without a look
Angry for all the time that it took
Now devil's eyes and an angel's heart
Digging deeper and deeper into the dark
Compensation to the minimum without a question
Life then death and now resurrection
Utopian people with Hell's mind
Twenty-twenty eyesight, but forever so blind
Passing through, one by one, all just the same
Winning the race without anything to gain
Searching, forgetting, a finding in the matter
Insane with ideas now nicknamed the Mad Hatter
Hearts of hearts and souls of souls
Innocent lives the future stole
Turning on these simple minds
Walking on the hands of time
Running crooked circles around again
Grasping the final concept from within

"Too Much Unspoken"

The door was open with a slight glare
A child by appearance, an adult by stare
The history seen when you looked in her eyes
The unsettling feeling because she no longer cried
The unspoken words of a ripened soul
An extended life story, seventeen years full
Thoughts she should not be able to understand
They were everyday occurrences and to her quite bland
With nothing to show for all of her years of pain
Except scars and open wounds running down her veins
Feelings of anything right soon became impossible
Her self-inflicted pain could put you in the hospital
Seeing through broken glass living in a delusion
The book was finally written and had no conclusion
One knife, two wrists, no more time for admiration
She found an easy answer to her parentless equation

"Ignorant Maturity"

Can you read me, am I not able to deceive

Walking through mud with my soul on my sleeve

No ink blots can tell you what is wrong in my head

My sanity frantically evading the last hopeless thread

Naked to say what I really am and ashamed to feel

For the sake of my psychosis, I may not feel real

Fearful of consistency and expecting more problems

Slamming down my fist because I don't know what caused them

This relentless cancer that hides in the deepest part of my soul

Reactions that are triggered with every set of dice I roll

With a chance that one time they might be correct

I chose life to be a game and for that my mind is wrecked

Not sure how to turn back from where I am going

With hatred for myself still steadily flowing

Pain and terror shooting through this irregular heart that is torn

With reactions like a child from this fragile soul that was scorned

Death is soon to conquer, so I better get ready

I took too many pills, now my eyes are getting heavy

My health is dropping and my kidney's failing

Blood pressure rising and the train track derailing

Chilling with a beer in hand, coming closer to death

With a hit off my cigarette as I take my last breath

"Empty"

Hollowness welling up and filling you inside
The feeling when you smell death and can no longer cry
No accomplishment could ever fill that empty space
Whatever you had lost could not be replaced
Wanting to be alone with a notebook and a pencil
All emotions seem like they were made with the same stencil
How did any of this even start, this feeling of constant death
Yearning to take the final problem so you could take your last breath
People say that you runaway from the problems in your life
But you don't, there is still skin on your body for the slice of a knife
Unsociable to everyone, even your best friend
Figuring out if you should wait or make that feeling end

17 million people are affected by depression each year in the U.S.

"Hiding"

Underneath this hat that is never taken off her head

Is a mind that was ignored, therefore she feels half dead

Beneath these baggy clothes that have so much to conceal

Is a person that wants to talk to someone, so she can finally heal

The outside is tore up and on the inside she is dark

She used to have potential, enough to build Noah his arc

No one helped her put any thoughts into motion

No real ties to anything, but needing some form of devotion

Pain and aggression stacking up and reaching the final line

Becoming more fearless going through life racing every stop sign

Running out of outlets with every person she would pass

She saw a cliff while driving and slammed on the gas

"Whispers"

In the dark, pouring rain
Look in the mirror, now I am vain
A dark cloud, a faded light
Lightning flashes, light up the night
Blood is dripping, no real thoughts
No one noticed, until caught
Building a bridge, traffic in my head
Eyes aggressive, now turning blood red
Telling the truth, still feeling guilt
Pain is stretching, strength starts to wilt
Too many screams now solemn whispers
The burns were deep, so many blisters
The followers come, they all join
The whispers grow soft, they lost the point

"Help"

I wake up every afternoon and drag myself to the mirror
Hoping it won't be that bad this time, but I always have that fear
I take off my blood stained shirt and examine the damage
Then I try to fix it, hoping it doesn't need more than a bandage
I wonder how old I will be when I finally break this cycle
I do it every day now; I have needed this pain for a while
I wrote the word 'Help' on a letter no one will ever receive
Now I just lie here hoping I could be anyone but me
When I get ready to start at night, I pick the perfect spot
I wear long sleeves all the time so I don't get caught
Still no one has noticed which makes this easier on me
Because no one can see my weakness, I just don't want them to see
A shirt covers up the scars on my shoulders, arms, and chest
I put on a pair of jeans which will cover up the rest
Incapable of functioning like a normal human being
There must be something there that I'm just not seeing
Blood simply oozing down the top of my arm
Since no one can know the marks don't go too far
The few friends that found out asked why I do this to myself
The only response I have is it feels better than anything else

Self abusive behavior is estimated to affect 2 to 3 million Americans

"After Eternity"

Questioning life by the age of six or seven

Pondering the concepts about hell and heaven

More questions in her mind then she ever wanted to ask

By now she is sixteen and walking around with a mask

She was cutting through her pain with a dull tip

Getting sick if she drove too far or went away on a trip

This was not right since the last place she'd want to be is at home

That was the first reason she started writing these poems

Her mind and soul were fragile and no one knew

She hurt all of the time, nobody had a clue

Time prolonged and left her with few choices

That was when she started listening to the voices

Doing different things to relieve the pain

Watching dark red water circling the drain

The only thing she wanted out of life was to be loved

Her mind decomposed as she was thrown around and shoved

The only entertainment she has now is a family heirloom

Sitting on an empty shelf in her locked and padded room

"Truth Be Told"

Surrounded by so many faces, still I am all alone

Happy people about me, yet I am made of stone

Half-heartedness, I think I need some help

Millions of people near, but I am all by myself

Sitting up at night feeling that I'm the only one alive

If something does not happen soon, I may need revived

I tune in a radio station or sit and watch TV

But everyone is sleeping, everyone but me

I close my eyes and try to clear my head

3 a.m. rolls around as I lie across my bed

There are stains of blood everywhere and I don't even hide it

The blade is out every night, I no longer try to fight it

More and more keeps adding up and no one understands

Sometimes I feel as if I am in my own demented land

"Could You Imagine"

You slapped me, punched me, and emotionally screamed
Verbally rejecting every part of my being
You embarrassed me and almost beat me half to death
With bruises everywhere, there is no room left
I feel like a failure, you even cheated on my father
You told me that I was the world's worst daughter
Just one time you should have been in my shoes
Cutting away the pain, but what else could I do
You heard about me cutting and forced more emotional blows
You made fun of me for it and said it was just for show
Could you even imagine that much pain to inflict wounds on yourself
To drag a blade across your skin because of the way that you felt
I look in the mirror and cannot face the person looking back
So go ahead and yell or scream and make sure you stab me in the back

"The Reason I am"

The beautiful summer of nineteen ninety-one
Just six years old playing beneath the summer sun
At night were the only times that lead to fear
Not knowing how much worse it would be in a few years
You have become the salt entering my wound
Pushing me too soon out of my cocoon
Hearing your voice can now make me shiver
Owning up to being your child makes me quiver
I know what you are and I will call you a thief and a liar
With an outlook on life to be the match that lights the fire
So now open your ears and listen if you can
It is your turn to see my candy land
Every time you come back and act like you are there
Just remember the one kid that did not care
Anytime you hear about a mother that let her kids die
Remember how you made all of us feel inside
Whenever you hold all of the cards in your hand
Remember the royal flush that put you in quicksand
When you think I am being evil and extremely cold
Just remember you are the darkness within my soul
And every second when crack is on your mind
Just remember the family you left behind

"Addicted to the Pain"

The tears still fall so quietly caused by emotional strain
That is why I started; I began my addiction to the pain
With no one there to talk to because everyone was the same
That is why I continued my addiction to the pain
Drinking to hide myself away from all of the constant shame
I became addicted, addicted to the pain
Feeling trickles of blood flowing from all of my veins
I realized the obsession; I craved the addiction to the pain
Memories were branded leaving scars in my brain
Leaving me addicted, addicted to this pain
Hassling myself over every mistake leaving me so drained
Scared to leave my addiction, my addiction to the pain
More and more things happened and I was to blame
Without control over myself I am dealing with the pain
This made me feel better more than anything I obtained
That is why my soul died, addicted to the pain

"Beneath the Surface"

The happiest person to help another smile
Even if she had not smiled in a while
Can anyone remember the last time they had stopped by
Or been there on a bad day when she would start to cry
All the while no one knew how she was feeling
Her emotions let loose because she was constantly dealing
With her voice so silent, yet wanting to be heard
No one noticed her because she hadn't said a word
All alone in her room at night after all of the parties
No one ever questioned why she was absent or tardy
They assumed she cared less and that is why she is gone
Until the announcement on the speaker when it finally dawned
'Elizabeth died last night at midnight, due to blood loss
Now everyone realized how she paid the ultimate cost
When no one wants to care this is what happens
Everyone was there, but only when she was laughing
Nobody saw the abrasions or they did and said nothing
This all happened because of the day she started cutting

"Addiction"

Night after night sitting at the kitchen table

Trying to fight the urge, yet I am still unable

Living in this world of untold truth and realization

Not knowing if yesterday was real or just a hallucination

Staring at this open bottle looking me in the eyes

Irritated with myself because my actions come as no surprise

Feeling the alcohol ripple through my blood stream into my brain

Watching my color go pale and the reduction in my veins

How do you let something grab hold and never let go

This is definitely suicide, it's just happening too slow

Forgetting months and years, just skipping through the days

I grab just one more bottle then that one starts to cascade

Trying to break the habit is like never breaking it at all

Because a new fixation happens, therefore another brick wall

Alcoholics, drug addicts, gambling addiction, and so on

Living their lives for that moment and then the moments gone

1 in every 8 Americans has a drug or alcohol problem

It is estimated that 27 million Americans are heavy drinkers or use illicit drugs

"Miss You"

I dig my nails into the deepest part of my mental
Trying to collect my thoughts, but they are just rentals
Bits of me escaping remembering pieces of you
Feeling like something was wrong, but you left without a clue
I am standing in this bathtub with a radio and extension cord
I would have used pills, except this is all I could afford
You should not have come back, after all that you did to our name
Being addicted to the substance and pointing at us for the blame
Thinking about how you made my brothers and sister feel
I was heartbroken for them and to you it was no big deal
Was it that difficult to mutter the words I am sorry
This mess you call our lives is another pointless safari
Why did you make us the enemy when you should have loved us
Instead you fell susceptible to evil and threw us away for lust
You were supposed to defend us and believe in our dreams
One time you told me you would be there by any means
I must thank you for this life because now we are stronger
We will not waste our energy on missing you any longer

"Another Picture on the Wall"

Pain is no more and emotions are free
A time of guilt, sorrow, and empathy
Nineteen forever for that time was priceless
Remembrance overall has so much brightness
Old friends meet again and regret the lost time
Starting over and knowing everything will be fine
Broken families reunite and come together again
Crying on each others shoulders with a few close friends
Candle light vigils, flowers on a headstone
Memorials with pictures as long as they were known
People being mortal, yet memories never die
Regret with total agony to look down and see them cry
Shedding tears of unimportance for this persons soul
Damned forever down here in this six foot hole
Do not weep for her picture in the corner of your mirror
Cry for the waste of her nineteen years

"Haunted House"

The floors started breathing with an evil vibe
The skeletons our family ultimately denied
Blood trickled down from the hallway ceiling
Shadows in the backyard with an eerie feeling
Voices at night in the kitchen for the frightened
The demon in the closet had made our terror heighten
Coming out only when we were fast asleep
The spirit would tip toe through and slowly creep
Grabbing us at the first open chance he received
At first this couldn't be real, but then we believed
He told us his name in that demonic voice
What could we do, did we even have a choice
We looked and looked, but finally we found a new home
The first night was great until we were alone…

"Never Ending"

I cannot stop this pattern no matter what I hear

People see my scars and their eyes project fear

Suicide is the first thought inserted in their brain

That is not why, this is difficult to explain

I cannot express to the people that know, the sorrow I feel

When this first started, it was not that big of a deal

I try to be good, but I always end up in defeat

If good overshadows evil I must be the villain to beat

Dementia is not hard if you have never been in the spotlight

Living your days in darkness, even when it isn't night

I love my family and friends, but they are deaf to my voice

I do not know how to explain that I have no other choice

Please do not hate me for something I no longer can control

The knife is what grasped me and my life that it stole

I can cry no longer because I do not feel any pain

Trying to say why I do it, that is where I strain

I will try again tomorrow, but I am off to fantasy land now

I would love to live in reality, but even my parents forgot how

"Broken Soul"

I have found the answer and it was so effortless

Finally something clicked in my head, I cannot believe this

When I begin to mourn over nothing, the sun rises again

All of the sadness and aggression walks out and silence sets in

At this moment I would like to see someone try to read my soul

No one can because my bottle of emotions is too full

I wonder if my parents will ever admit their darkened pasts

Or actually try to give us the life they never had

I am not speaking about money and material possessions

Just give us advice or guidance, even teach us a lesson

You both made our lives worse then yours ever could have been

Teaching us nothing except the best ways to sin

Maybe you should give us possessions; at least they have a warranty

They promise if the product is corrupt we get money back guarantee

I hate to talk about my parents in the ways that I do

If they acted different then this would not have to be true

I guess I am supposed to be the parent and the mediator

Stopping the kids from fighting and buying food for the refrigerator

I am becoming so exhausted from being what everyone wanted me to be

That I forgot who I was, my life has become a technicality

"Out of Time"

Blame cannot be placed on anyone for the life that was wasted

Only one person must have the guts to come up and face it

I could have said no to the bad choices I made, but now I am stuck

All the bad I have done leaves me feeling responsible for my bad luck

Out of time because I am starring at my twenty-two

With no one to place blame on, Mom, not even you

I decided my own fate the second I picked up my gun

In school I was asked about my future and knew I never had one

Now the sweat masking my body like a rainy mist

I know friends will be upset for the years I will miss

They shed a few tears, but really it is just a guilty mind

Putting it in the past and leaving me behind

Now no one has to worry or be taken by surprise

No more harm to my body and no more risking D. U. I. 's

My life turned out how everyone expected, no more reason to wonder

I was always close to death and he finally called my number

"Who Cares"

I will no longer be the composer of self-loathing criticism
I will avenge my soul and charge my mind with plagiarism
This post mortem feeling eating away inside of me
With treacherous pains just yearning to break free
The walls have layered over the years of disclosure
My mental capacity has perceptions boiling over
No more I continue saying, yet I will not talk
I stepped back for a moment and my whole life was docked
Forsaken dreams have come out, I just need a connection
Collisions of tears and rain caused the emotional infection
No one has ever wondered why nobody sees me smiling
Someone hold me tight because I keep on declining
I can still feel the aftermath of my own defeat
Until I am done typing and then press delete

"I Try Not To"

I try to think God may have mercy every once in a while

Then another situation happens to put us back a couple of miles

If it isn't death, then it is drugs breathing in our face

We may have a moment of solitude then Satan gives us a taste

I try not to let anyone hurt or to be in need

Yet there is only so much that I can personally bleed

I am trying, yet I am dying and no one knows right now

They will wait until I am gone and the coroner can explain how

I will teach as well as I can before I disappear

Hoping that when I am gone they will still feel me near

They just need some guidance until the end of my days

But who am I to think they should listen to someone holding a blade

The one that cut me so deep that it did not even bleed

Making me feel even lower which is the only thing I don't need

All I ask for now is for my siblings to make it in this life

Deal with your problems, but do not focus on the strife

Take the breathes I never felt and the steps I could not take

Just please live a life and do not make the same mistakes

"Statistic"

Just when she thought anything horrible had been thrown at her
Almost the biggest destroyer ever left her in a lifelong blur
Left with thinking thoughts her mind constantly produced
Recalling that night over and over with only the devil amused
Not wanting to see it again, but it would not go away
Cringing at the terrible thoughts that her mind wanted to replay
She could not explain the feeling of the images she fought
Feeling like less of a person with each second she thought
Flashbacks would happen and she would instantly freeze
She cried and struggled wondering 'Why did this happen to me'
Why did she feel like pushing away everyone that cared
Suffering in silence because she was trembling and scared
Shutting down her system so no one could hurt her again
Words from a mask she used on all of her friends
Depression showed up first and then came denial
She was too terrified to even put this man on trial
She thought 'this would never happen to me'
As she became a statistic for the whole world to see

1 in 6 women…

1 in 33 men…

Are sexually assaulted in their life

"Sick of being the victim"

Lying naked in the city, completely exposed
It's cold and everyone is layered, but I have no clothes
I look at all the people with their coats and hats
Yet I am alone only dreaming I could be like that
No matter how many times I shower I will never be clean
To ever feel whole again is only in my dreams
I try to accomplish so much, but it's not at all for my sake
I just need to constantly move whenever I am awake
Silence couldn't stop everyone from knowing what I am
Afraid to meet new people because they might know that man
The beast that made me this way, scared to even venture outside
Making it hard to get up in the morning because relief would be to die
I have more depressing episodes than I ever have before
Knowing that everyone sees me and I know they think I'm a whore
I wish I could sleep all the time and never have to wake up
But he is even in there, so alcohol overflows my cup
At times drinking makes me forget, but sometimes it gets worse
No matter how many I have I cannot seem to quench this thirst
My parents didn't help me and my older brother said I was lying
Yet they all want to know why all I think about is dying

"His Face"

Contemplating whether what happened was truth or a lie
If it was not true, why did thinking of it tear her up inside
Did she deceive the uninformed minds around her
'Unfortunately it is true' as she thought how it occurred
The night was eerie and she felt scared of what would take place
She thinks about it every minute, trying to forget his face
Shaking and terrified, she tries to put it out of her mind
Then that face appears with a look so unkind
No one was told at first, hoping it would erase
But once her eyes are closed there again is his face
Did it paralyze him as much as it did her
No, that question was the first adjourned
She will not face it, but that is how to put it all behind
Rape has put pain, anger, and fear inside her tangled mind

"Manically Depressed"

I had a flashback and could not come back
My memory was slow, but time went fast
No one believed me, I was against the world
I wanted to go back to being a little girl
I was so strong, but became so weak
I am crying so hard, I can't even speak
My head is pounding and I am so tired
Maybe I'll quit my job or try and get fired
If I don't even like me, how could anyone else
Showing empathy to the world, but none for myself
I wanted a mom, just once so she could hug me
Time and time again, no one there to love me
Death would be welcome after I crawl into a hole
It would be so much easier than exposing my soul
Someone come and save me because I know I won't
Wait a minute, on second thought, please just don't

60% of sexual assaults are not reported

"Sunday Morning"

I tried to end it all Sunday, but I don't know why
My brain is forever programmed to overdose and die
If this is a mental disorder, then I cannot be helped
But if I could not help it would I still end up in hell
I know who I really am and that was not me that day
Someone else took over; I was a puppet in a play
Now nobody believes me and they think I need treatment
Maybe I should just go before I cause anyone else bereavement
Time keeps ticking by, yet my life has been stopped
I sit alone saturated in the sound of this damn clock
I want to shatter my mirror or break through my kitchen wall
Because I do not know what to do, how far will I fall
It is selfish for me to kill myself because of friends and family
But isn't it selfish of them to keep me here if I don't want to be
The psychiatrist made me worse, counseling worked for a while
Now my mind is on the stand, but my body is at trial
I cannot let my brain keep testifying against me
Because it caused the bloodshed that was almost as big as the sea
My body was found guilty and my mind laughed and walked away
As I was rejected on my last appeal I now had a permanent stay

"No One to Remember Her"

Life would be easier if she did not feel this way

She would be a leader instead of being the prey

Blood red sickness inside her eyes

She became the person that she despised

No one cares about her, so she no longer mattered

When she tried to take a step up, she got pushed off her ladder

She is alone when she screams late at night

Walking away from any type of spotlight

Her scars will heal and her wounds will mend

Even if they don't, she will just pretend

Hell could not make her feel any phonier

All she wanted was to talk, but she died even lonelier

She never knew how to be around others or how to connect

She was here for a reason and that was to protect

But no one would protect her, she saw it all

Living as an adult of 14, not surviving the free fall

As her time here comes down to one last fight

The thought of living makes her chest grow tight

She will not be remembered as the protector, just the one who lost

Living in Hell with her soul being the only cost

"My Toast to Death"

I can still taste you, see you, and feel you
I still see your face with every day that accrues
Every guy has a feature that terrifies my mind
They look like you, forcing me to drink until I'm blind
I hate the embarrassment I feel, so I lie to everyone
Telling them I'm okay and acting like I'm having fun
A permanent smile on my face with sad eyes to contrast
Partying every weekend, forging excitement is a task
Young kids think I'm a rebel, while adults just look away
Therefore I hold a beer to my lips with nothing vital to say
I study hard in college, but for what I do not know
By the time I am thirty, I will have performed my final show
Drinking one too many times and always acting real funny
Until one fateful night when I will have brought too much money
I will have a few too many drinks and invincible I will become
Never realizing my drunken antics were always incredibly dumb
Whether I get behind the wheel or get thrown through some glass
Perhaps I will get shot in a parking lot or jump from the overpass
I will always have known one memory to be true
I could still taste you, see you, and feel you

"Down Fall"

A simple plan of life without a detour
But I am going in circles, I have seen this all before
The same false arrest under the broken down tree
The sun and the moon circling around the deep blue sea
Another speeding ticket along with a court case
Sending the lawyers on another wild goose chase
Knee deep in emotional debt and still walking
My mouth finally opened, yet still no talking
I thought you would be my rock, but you got in my way
Left without an answer, all I can do is pray
Once again no response, I must be doing it wrong
I am still a teenager and my life is already too long
Sell me short because my negativity needs another lift
Throw me the wrapping paper without giving me the gift
Standing on the tracks and the light is getting closer
It was too late for me, I fell off the roller coaster

"Why"

Why do I say all of the things that I say

Why does it always rain on my parade

Why do I have so many dreadful memories

Why do I always seem to have the wrong chemistry

Why do I have nightmares when I close my eyes

Why am I always brought down by my own demise

Why did we have to be the poorest family in town

Why can't I write a book someone doesn't want to put down

Why am I up late at night thinking too much

Why do I hate emotions and the human touch

Why am I terrified to be submerged in water

Why do I feel like such a horrible daughter

Why do I drink if I am going to black out

Why do I whisper when I know I should shout

Why must I bottle up my emotions inside

Why can't I write a poem that does not rhyme

All of the why's without any reasons

More questions forming with the changing seasons

"Childlike Reaction"

Air is still filling your lungs, but you are dead
Causing chills running down my spine while I lie awake in bed
I may have before, but cannot love you anymore
Since my 15th birthday you never stepped foot through the door
I never really expected you to and now I don't know what to do
I am broken, my body is scarred, and this all started with you
It would be too soon if I never saw your face again
Uncontrollable rage seems to be my new life's trend
No person in my life will have ever treated me so bad
Stealing from my family and cheating on my dad
Pops started drinking again while you were out messing around
I will never be content until you are six feet underground
Well maybe somewhere else as long as you're not around me
The judge could put you in prison and throw away the key
Because anytime you are around my mind begins to rain
I am only eighteen and you have left me utterly drained
I will never love because the only result is pain
I picked up your slack and all you did was complain
I cannot take your mood swings anymore and I will not have to
Just wait and see because you have no idea what I can do

"What I Was Before"

Do you still remember how we used to be

Daddy's girl forever, at least that's what it was to me

We would go to the mall and I would hold your hand

That time seems gone forever, like an hour glass without sand

I no longer know what is truth or what is fiction

I could care less if anyone could give me a fine prediction

Now all that echoes are the broken promises made

With all the good memories starting to fade

I saw you then as my hero, never in the wrong

Playing sports or riding your dirt bikes all day long

On vacation I would tag along following your footsteps

With an admiration for you that reached unthinkable depths

You never realized that you were my shining star

Wanting to be like you even when times became hard

Then you started deceiving me like I was stupid, flipping my world around

This was the final straw, with a gun in hand my soul was never found

I couldn't take it anymore; both parents started telling me lies

Life insurance will provide for the kids and they will no longer cry

I used to be a daddy's girl, but something must have happened

Killing him and mom, in a straight jacket now I'm laughing

**It is estimated that 11 million children under 18
live with parents that are alcoholics**

"Goodbye"

Thoughts arising in this brain that feels so cursed

Considering life or death and which one is worse

Friends leave me feeling distant, but I never wanted them to go

They are there for the moment and then leave after the show

Feelings of anguish and tribulation are in the midst

If anymore happens, then death may be my only kiss

Love is a word I no longer use since it has been aborted

Ever since then reality has been cold and distorted

Why must existence linger over our simple minds

Patiently waiting for death to conquer, just waiting for that time

These thoughts unspoken are why we feel so hollow inside

Not wanting to think about the last time we'll have to say goodbye

"Trying, but…"

Seduced by minor casualties

Ignoring the true realities

Having a dream so big that is it, just a dream

Getting frustrated so my tears become an endless stream

Lingering on every word that it is unreal

Careless in the way that she wants to appeal

Just let go of all the stresses, yet it is so hard

They say 'reach for the stars,' but she can't make it that far

She never knew positivity and still cannot face it

Rather feeling that if she failed she would have a replacement

Thinking as if her existence is like a grain of sand on the beach

Billions more are there and she isn't significant enough to be reached

Now a sickness starts in her mind, too overwhelming to conceal

Randomly she prays with tear drops falling as she kneels

Asking God to help her gain strength, truth, and understanding

It's like she has been flying forever and cannot find a landing

"Suicidal"

Sleeping through school, working all night

Walking home in the dark, trying to stay in the light

All that time to think creates an act of indecency

Feelings of grave confusion and total complexity

Life has made feelings into words indescribable

Yearning for the human body to be free of it's soul

Fast and painless are the feelings wanted

Words for the final letters are still being hunted

The universe started spinning in the wrong direction

Turning me to stone, so I have no more affection

The skies turned gray and tornado season started

Trying to stop visualizing my body being carted

Sweating then freezing, this is like a sickness

Not caring about the good times that I'm going to miss

No one seemed to wonder at any time throughout my past

About why I am like this, the first stone has been cast

I grew up thinking I would not make it to the age of eighteen

The time is right, the mood is set, now I must make the scene

32,439 people committed suicide in 2004

Statistics showed that this was the 11th leading cause of death in the US

"Dead All Along"

My soul slipped out so there was no one left to resuscitate
The paramedics finally arrived thirty seconds too late
The satanic desire for death was filled, which stopped the yearning
The tears I used to cry died down so my eyes quit burning
The darkness finally swallowed the nightmare I was living in
I was calm now with the last dose of misery conquering within
Everyone expected me to do it, but no one was ready
I pulled the blade across, my hand perfectly steady
As the life drained out of me I was glad to see the verdict
I would have shot myself but someone might have heard it
I tried to fight the battles which left wounds on my extremities
I wanted to cure myself, but used all of the wrong remedies
I was so tired and now I can finally sleep for all eternity
Yet I am still praying for death, what the hell is wrong with me
I remember the night I died; I can see it so clearly
I must have been dead already, the living dead no one could see
Now I am stuck walking this earth forever living in a state of fatigue
I know in life I was correct, I must have been out of my league

"Getting Under my Dead Skin"

I don't believe in antidepressants, so this is the result
Found and initiated, I am stuck in my own cult
Counselors make me crazier so I talk to myself
I've never been materialistic and could care less about my health
Ignore me like you have always done for so many years
Tell me how I'm worthless now because I'm just shifting gears
If God is supposed to be my oh so everlasting
And be the filling of my hunger then I must be fasting
Hypocritical of my life, when you came from nothing too
So forget what you say I'm just setting out for what I have to do
Going off the deep end is an understatement
My mind is a mansion, but I can't get out of the basement
I'm sick of you telling me that my problem is my drinking
I learned this from you, what the hell are you thinking
Inject me slowly with happiness and I will probably overdose
Maybe I'll take some sleeping pills and set my mind on coast
Unconventionally I laugh in my warped and paralyzed mind
Over and over bad memories, but you keep pressing rewind
Can't you see you are stepping right onto my soul
Leaving me with so much pain and no one tries to console
I cannot live listening to the things you have to say
Can you please just let me sleep, even just for today

"Angel's Wings"

Too many stories, but none honestly matter

She is frozen in the past, touch her heart and she will shatter

Laughter last century and pain in the next

The luckiest of days still seemed to be hexed

Sorrows of joy and joys of sorrow

Living by the day, no more happy tomorrows

Evil inside just waiting to come out

Yet holding it back, trying not to have doubt

Days pass and soon they turn into years

Loosing in life, screaming bloody tears

No one knew why all of a sudden she cried

The part of her life that decided not to die

The alcohol level was at zero, but she was acting insane

She lost at what she was playing and life was her game

Finally death arrived, but she ended up in hell for many things

Now she will never know what it's like to fly with Angel's wings

"Someone Simply Love Me"

To hurt in solemn silence for the day to finally come
The point in time when anyone could tell me why I'm numb
To not just mask the pain and embarrassment, but make it evade my depth
Someone to wipe away each tear drop I have ever wept
Accepting the past and refilling my heart after the dehydration of my soul
Drenched in pain, screaming from the tears, I will do anything to feel whole
With my abandoned past resurfacing and a insightful person there to help
I can finally say these words 'I can no longer do this by myself'
If someone was there and I could stop pushing people away
Maybe love would not be so hard to feel or so difficult to say
Perhaps if almost every person wouldn't have turned their backs
Or maybe if I was not brought up on the wrong side of the tracks
With cultivating memories echoing, there are too many to list
With excruciating thoughts that make me not want to exist
I need someone to help me feel like a real person
To escape life for a while and my latest diversion
I want to feel what it is like to have an angel above me
Another day has passed, one more day no one has loved me

"Aimless Boulevard"

Farewell to the memories that have tried to escape
For these eternal walls will not let them flake
To wake up in sorrow each time I have the urge to breathe
Even my subconscious knows, but I just can't believe
Toying with every thought of what I have become
With a relinquished past which is what I branch from
Haunting me for the depth in which I had it buried
We were the innocents, but our parent's mistakes we had carried
Childhood is a mistake that leaves a lifetime of corrections
I started down the right road and then I lost the directions
Misty eyed I ponder on the thoughts of my youth
Lonely and scared even as I lost my first tooth
A mind of disenchantment through quiet intelligence
Wondering how rich you had to be for stresses to relent
As I get older and we get poorer I begin to realize
Wealth is different in every person's eyes
Money can take away problems that poverty cannot
So many have succeeded and the little people they forgot
Weary of the wealthy because many have not treated me right
So I step off my pedestal before I remember my fear of heights
Being a good person is difficult if you do not hold the cards
Thus I stroll so aimlessly walking down the boulevard

"I apologize"

I apologize to my family, for that I am not wrong

I apologize to you for saying you don't belong

I apologize for myself for the sympathy I have for you

I apologize for my younger siblings, because they bestow that too

I apologize to myself for my ability of love unconditionally

I apologize to my older brother for supporting us financially

I am sorry for the drinking and same games everyday

I apologize for all the disappointing things that I say

Forgive me for each of my stupid choices and actions

I am sorry for every time I had a mother-like reaction

I can say these words over and over until the end

I apologize until we see our new lives begin

I apologize for you not having any emotional ties

Instead of being our mother you gave us the fight of our lives

"Fade Away"

One day your life will finally fade away
Decomposing from every excuse you ever made
By the time you read this your life will have no definition
Living like you always did, without any prohibitions
Thinking about my family hurts me fiercely inside
Realizing no one would care if any of us lived or died
Yet we stepped up and tried so hard to keep everyone together
One family, half a parent, substantially forever
I just wish we were the reason you wanted to breathe
But we all know that drugs are a bigger necessity
We must break away from the life you no longer try to hide
Remembering the past pain, but we no longer cry
No more lies, no more stealing, or fighting to be seen
I gave up a long time ago on seeing you get clean

"Barely Getting By"

As I bleed to death on the floor, I don't even scream
I lost the ability to feel pain so I am living in a dream
No matter how many cuts I make or beers I drink, I am still dead
I start drinking even more until there is a bullet in my head
I am no longer a child, so I should know how to deal
Angry voices in my mind are telling me how to feel
They tell me bad things about all the people I have met
Leaving me paranoid and in a constant cold sweat
I got off the highway of emotion and drove into crazy town
I am the only one here and I do not hear a sound
I want to go home, but no one is there
I was rejected by the people that were supposed to care
Now blood is splashing into the core of my brain
Slowly filling up, my body is finally tame
I feel the pain in my mind and hear the voice of treason
I sentenced myself to death for no apparent reason

"Depression"

I once thought depression was just a big joke
Now I walk around carrying Satan's cloak
Perhaps we are all victims between depression's claws
Mine started when I began thinking about my flaws
Everyone always said that you couldn't even tell
They never knew that my life was like a living Hell
I wonder if life has shown me too much like over exposure
Like people going to calling hours and they say it's for closure
I am not seeking pity, even though it may seem I might
I write because I am alone and cannot sleep at night
The sun will begin to set and my world becomes a dark zone
Then the sky grows darker with an ecstatic purple tone
Shadows start to appear without anyone to be seen
Sometimes there are voices and other times a dream
This is why I spend the majority of my life awake
Now I wish depression really was fake

Rape victims are:

3 times more likely to suffer from depression

6 times more likely to suffer from Post Traumatic Stress Disorder

"Prosperity Perhaps"

I have been screaming for help silently forever
Pain and humiliation always seem to work together
Now that help has shined its face I feel awkward and racy
To understand how to look at myself and actually face me
To not always look down if I talk about my problems
Instead of drinking them down I could actually solve them
I am terrified, palms sweating, my mind keeps thinking
No moisture in my eyes whenever I am blinking
Perhaps I could trust someone, but what if I am wrong
What if they end up treating me like everyone else has all along
Maybe a last chance for life and perhaps it could be
To no longer hide in darkness, but feel happy and free
I want to laugh without sadness, but I never knew how
Hopefully to unhappiness this will be my last bow

"Selfishness"

I weep at night thinking about the dire things I have done
The person saying vulgar things and drinking, I was that one
I care more about my family than myself or anybody
I would help my brother's with their homework before I would study
I still cannot figure out why I am so hard on myself
Criticizing and judging me more than anyone else
I look in the mirror and cannot figure out why
Anyone would think I'm beautiful, let alone a handsome guy
Friends have told me different, but I still feel insignificant
Feeling like a good person is a statement that is insufficient
Whenever I talk about my problems, I think I am being conceded
I even feel like this when I write poems about how I was treated
Believing that everyone has life worse off than me
Leads me to keep silent about my own life story
I am about to change that, I will not keep quiet any longer
Because everyday I live makes me that much stronger
Reaching out to children is the new reason for my poems
At least then they might not wake up like me, feeling all alone

"Lonely Defiance"

I am trying to hold on, but my hands are slipping from this earth
Starting in the middle of 1999 the year our emotions disbursed
Trying to stabilize my life and have just one consistency
Telling friends around me, yet no one believed me
I have always needed help and I always pushed it away
I know I have problems, what more can I say
There is one person inside me that wants to guide this train wreck
But I am the conductor and do not know how to direct
I start to learn on my own and have personal experience
Instead of drinking all of the time and acting delirious
I am starting to realize how to be a better human being
To open my eyes and see what most are incapable of seeing
I want to look in the mirror and say nice things to myself
Because it is harder for me to say that then to anyone else
The days pass by and I am still my own worst enemy
I try to remember if I have ever been genuinely happy
One day at a time is how I am told to deal with things
Well are two or three days an option for what the future brings
I am trying to deal with one problem, but more get in the way
So I slow down and do what friends tell me, take it day by day

"Protector"

Going back in time to stand next to you

Protecting you from the people that lost life's pursuit

I will protect you from your parents or friends if need be

As long as you always remember you can count on me

Forgive the ones that made you go through torture for no purpose

Because they were drowning in sorrows and couldn't reach the surface

They would hit you or call you derogatory names

Acting like you should have to walk through hell's flames

You would hit them back and say self defense, but no one would listen

Now I am here to wipe away the tears that made your cheeks glisten

I will come take you away and help you deal with your pain

The way a child should, so they don't feel insane

You can scream at me if that will make you feel better

Just try to let it out, even if you have to write it in a letter

I want to give you a life that is not so crazy

Showing you that you can always be someone's baby

With absolute love that will always be true

Believing in you no matter what you do

As hard as this may be, you will finally believe

That there are people that give rather than receive

Just let me know when you are upset and I will be there

We can talk or I will listen, just know that I care

"They Are Safe Now"

You were the first person to ever make me see stars
You hit me in the face with your car keys leaving disturbing scars
Children Services turned me away and for that I had to run
I was only sixteen, but with life I was done
You made me hate my body, personality, and voice
Pushing me to the edge, until I did not have a choice
You called my twelve year old sister a bitch and a whore
From that moment on, I knew you would not hurt her anymore
I grabbed you from behind and choked you until you dropped
That was the day the child abuse had to be stopped
Anytime I was home and I heard the children scream
I followed their cries; it was like a demented dream
You would be running after them with fear on their little faces
I would beat you down because I knew I could never erase this
How could you do that, they were so tiny and scared
Looking at you as a giant, you were supposed to care
You beat the hell out of us and took advantage of our trust
You could not stand your children and abuse became a must
The little ones are safe now and their trust is gaining speed
And life seems worthwhile anytime they say they love me

4 children died everyday in 2006 from child abuse

3 out of 4 were under the age of 4

"Behind these Walls"

Stuck in this little room inside my skull
Emotions welling up incapable of breaking these walls
Pounding at my head again and again
Not able to break through my tattered skin
Running in circles, never wanting to stop
Paralyzed at the bottom, never reaching the top
Endless spirals of thoughts and feelings out of control
An entire world around me, but I am not whole
Bars that are locked tight, no sunlight to be seen
Everyone is gone; my bars are made of broken dreams
Hoping the last breath will be coming quite soon
My heart rate is slowing down, so out of tune
Until one special person walked through these bars
They saw into my soul, past all of my scars
Listening and sharing, helping me try to console
Never ending positivity that is uniquely unconditional
They gave me the key now that my heart and mind have risen
Now no one can lock me down in my own prison

"Substantially Forever"

The sole obsession to believe in one desire
Life's contract becomes burnt without using fire
The recent choice of decisions now truly demonic
Digging further and deeper with each sip of tonic
Running circles only in thought, yet mine are paralyzed
Objecting to everyone because of how I was characterized
Thoughts conquering to the maximum without resolution
The story of my life with a hollow conclusion
Twisted, spinning, the universe disengaged
All the while only the sane ones were enraged
This material country, how can you survive
If you don't live for money, then how are you alive
Well my planet is not set on the strong lines of perfection
The act of that is just a transparent deception
How is life to be lived if never lived at all
To live for the laughs and laugh at the falls

"Stuck in the Moment"

The days go by when I remember
Times of my youth, starting school in September
Baseball and football from dawn until dusk
No real guidance, so sticking together was a must
Our group had a bond, baseball games lasting forever
Summer days were eternal as long as we were together
Walking around town without money in our pockets
Friendships so tight that no one could unlock it
Everyone was vital and unique, no one was left out
Together we were happy, that was all that we were about
Friends forever was said and to that we stayed loyal
Whether we were having fun or making each other's blood boil
Your time with me was special and will always be eternal
Because my family and friends are the consistencies in my journal
We were always there during the good times and depressed
Whether we were playing ball together or being placed under arrest
Having each others friendship kept us all solid
Friends, buds, or pals; whatever it was that we called it

"Smiles"

A look back at past friends that had cared

People with fond memories that were openly shared

Too much happened at once now I am wondering where you went

Recalling every second that we had ever spent

Standing across from you, but I can see inside

Death, sadness, and addictions that start to subside

Going without a question to prepare the coming

The reincarnation of ourselves from when we were slumming

With everyday life you used to be the only color

Living life in shades rather then any other

Burning feelings remembering how we used to laugh

Tear drops falling as I stare at your photograph

Laughter is echoing from when were joking

Now we have quick responses, speaking before choking

Trying not to recall the bad days or the past trials

Making life worthwhile when we can make each other smile

"Living for Yourself"

Growing up around kids that had ideas of being invincible

Most went through life having everything except principles

Then there were the ones from the wrong side of the tracks

Fighting every day and always being held back

No one understood why they hated thinking about tomorrow

Nobody cared about them so they were left to drown in their sorrows

These are the kids that do not think they will live to see eighteen

That age comes and goes and now twenty-one becomes a dream

Not making any plans to hang out next month or even next week

Either acting out or very quiet because there is no reason to speak

Becoming an unnoticed master at school, music, or even art

Their parents do not care, since they have not from the start

Then there are parents more focused on school then emotional well being

As long as they have a diploma there is no reason for expressing feelings

Children need to take time out to live for the life that is still here

Do not think about parent's approval or the things they hold dear

We live for ourselves and that is all we can be asked to do

To wake up alive and do the things that we want to pursue

"Exhale"

I realize the effort it takes to care, but why do I not see it that way

I love my friends and family, but it's hard for me to wake up today

I do it anyway because I know that no one else will be there

Giving out lunch money, dressing them, or styling their hair

I went to bed a child and woke up like a mother of three

Instead of my dad teaching me to be grown, I taught him how to be

I get exhausted taking care of the kids and finding the houses we live in

Trying to teach them stability, which was a lesson I was never given

No wonder I don't take care of myself through all of these pointless trials

Searching online for a crisis hotline, but the number was never dialed

I am exhausted, but people depend on me to make the needed corrections

To take an interest in how they feel and sometimes show them affection

If I could only be like my dad who comes and goes at any time

Would he even care if he knew the thoughts burning in my mind

I remember being scared when dad went to jail for drunk driving

No adults were left at home which left my younger sister crying

By eighteen I knew I drank too much, but mom was so much worse

Murderous drug withdraw, raging paranoia, and brutal outbursts

The sleepless nights we had because no one felt safe at home

Fourteen years and younger, almost every night all alone

I remember my sister's isolation and my brothers crying so hard

The late night walks home from work because mom stole our car

The childhood I will never forget, thanking god that I'm now older

I finally obtained the help I needed so the world was lifted off my shoulders

"Parental Advisory"

Some of the words I used in this book are just for thought provoking purposes. I do not condone murder, suicide, drug abuse, self harming, underage drinking, or violence. I went through most of these events and made it out alive so that I could tell my story to help others. This book is simply to express the feelings I had growing up in the warped world I lived in. Please do not try to imitate anything you read here. If you or someone you know already has any of the problems mentioned in this book please go to my website and click on the 'Remedy' tab for information on how you or your friend or family member can be helped. If you would like to contact me to share a comment, question, or your own story my email address is listed below. Thank you for your support.

Website: **Dementeddreamz.net**

Email Address: **Dementeddreamzpoet@yahoo.com**

Statistics gathered from the following sources:

www.abovetheinfluence.com/facts/drugs-alcohol April 2003
www.childhelp.org/resources/learning-center/statistics 2006
www.coachinginternational.com/stats
www.healthline.com/galecontent/depression-1 2005
www.hopenetworks.org/addiction/Children%20of%20Addicts 2005
www.nimh.nih.gov/health/publications/suicide-in-the-us-statistics-and-
prevention/index 2004
www.rainn.org/statistics 2008
www.surgeongeneral.gov/library/mentalhealth/home
www.teenhelp.com/teen-health/cutting-stats-treatment 2009
www.wbko.com/news/headlines/17221439

www.ingramcontent.com/pod-product-compliance
Lightning Source LLC
Chambersburg PA
CBHW030156070426
42447CB00031B/683